FINGERPICKING
ELTON JOHN

Arrangements by Bill LaFleur

Cover photo by Jack Robinson/Hulton Archive/Getty Images

ISBN 978-1-4950-9762-1

HAL•LEONARD®

7777 W. BLUEMOUND RD. P.O. BOX 13819 MILWAUKEE, WI 53213

Visit Hal Leonard Online at
www.halleonard.com

Bennie and the Jets

Words and Music by Elton John and Bernie Taupin

Copyright © 1973 UNIVERSAL/DICK JAMES MUSIC LTD.
Copyright Renewed
This arrangement Copyright © 2018 UNIVERSAL/DICK JAMES MUSIC LTD.
All Rights in the United States and Canada Controlled and Administered by UNIVERSAL - SONGS OF POLYGRAM INTERNATIONAL, INC.
All Rights Reserved   Used by Permission

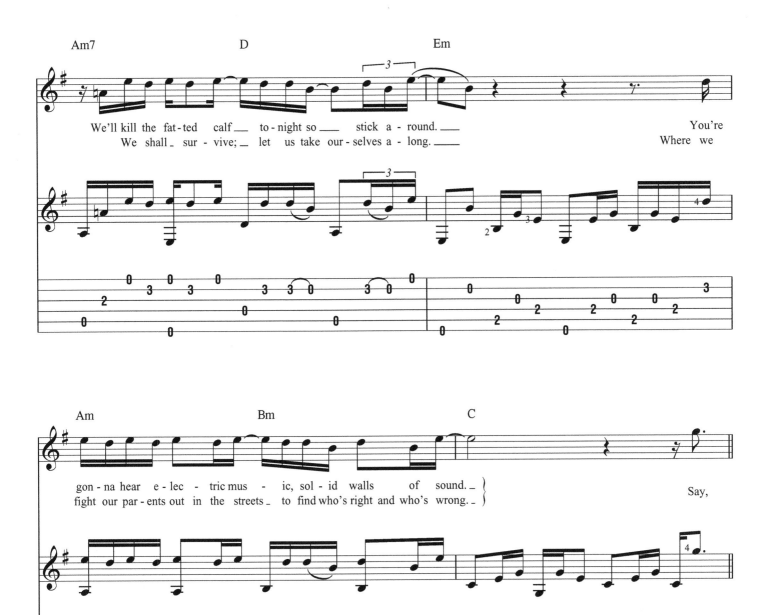

We'll kill the fat-ted calf __ to-night so __ stick a-round. __ You're
We shall __ sur-vive; __ let us take our-selves a-long. __ Where we

gon-na hear e-lec-tric mus - ic, sol-id walls of sound. __
fight our par-ents out in the streets __ to find who's right and who's wrong. __ Say,

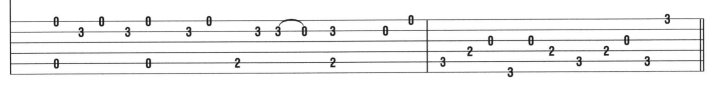

%. **Chorus**

Can-dy and Ron - nie, have you seen them yet? __ Ooh, but they're so __ spaced out, B - B - B - B - B -

Ben-nie and the Jets. Oh, ___ but they're weird ___ and they're won-der-ful. ___ Oh, Ben-

- nie she's ___ real-ly keen. She's got e-lec-tric boots, ___ a mo-hair suit, ___ you know I

read it in a mag-a-zine, ___ oh, ___ B - B - B - Ben-nie and the

2nd time, D.S. al Coda   ⊕ Coda

Outro

Border Song

Words and Music by Elton John and Bernie Taupin

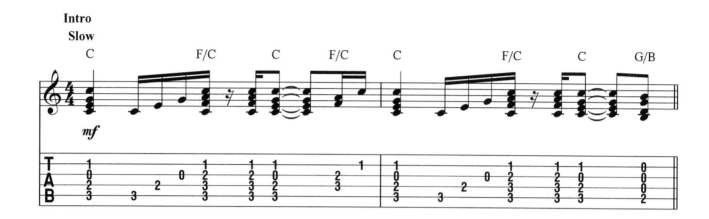

1. Ho - ly Mo - ses, _____ I have been __ re - moved. _____
2. Ho - ly Mo - ses, _____ I have been __ de - ceived. _____
3. Ho - ly Mo - ses, _____ let us live __ in peace. _____

I have seen __ the spec - ter, he has __ been __ here, too. __
Now the wind has changed di - rec - tion and I ____ have __ to __ leave. __
Let us strive __ to find a way to make all ___ ha - tred __ cease. __

Dis - tant cous - in from down the line, brand of peo - ple who ain't
Won't you please ex - cuse my frank - ness, but it's not my cup
There's a man o - ver there; what's his col - or? I

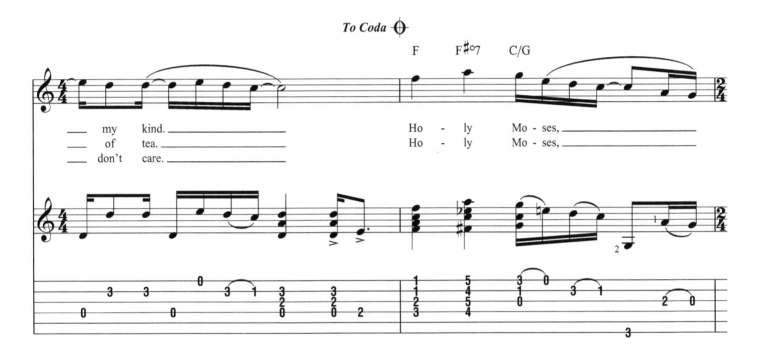

To Coda ⊕

my kind. Ho - ly Mo - ses,
of tea. Ho - ly Mo - ses,
don't care.

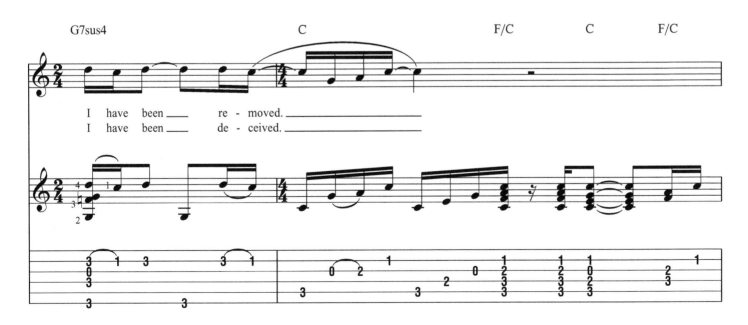

I have been re - moved.
I have been de - ceived.

I'm go - ing

Bridge

back to the bor - der where my af - fairs, where my af - fairs ain't a - bused.

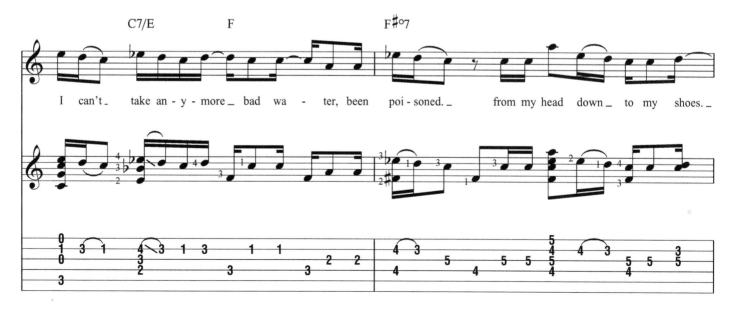

I can't take an - y - more bad wa - ter, been poi - soned. from my head down to my shoes.

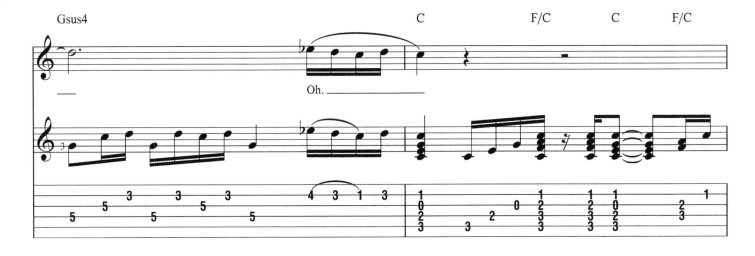

D.S. al Coda

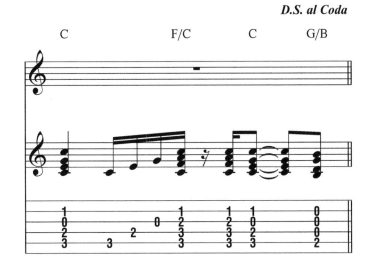

⊕ **Coda**

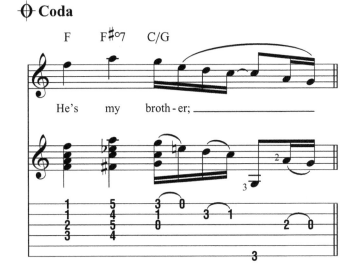

He's my broth-er; ___

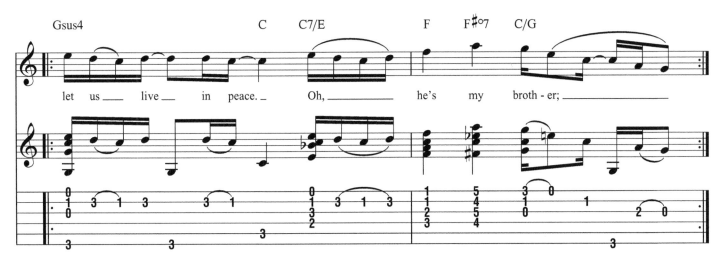

let us ___ live ___ in peace. ___ Oh, ___ he's my broth-er; ___

Slower

let us, ___ let us ___ live in peace. ___

Candle in the Wind

Words and Music by Elton John and Bernie Taupin

Verse
Moderately

1. Good-bye, Nor - ma Jean. Though I nev - er knew you at all,
2., 3. *See additional lyrics*

you had the grace to hold your - self while those a - round you crawled.

They crawled out of the wood - work,

Copyright © 1973 UNIVERSAL/DICK JAMES MUSIC LTD.
Copyright Renewed
This arrangement Copyright © 2018 UNIVERSAL/DICK JAMES MUSIC LTD.
All Rights in the United States and Canada Controlled and Administered by UNIVERSAL - SONGS OF POLYGRAM INTERNATIONAL, INC.
All Rights Reserved   Used by Permission

and they whis-pered in - to your brain. They set you on the tread-

- mill, and they made you change your name. And it

Chorus

seems to me you lived your life like a can - dle in the wind,

never know-ing who to cling to when the rain

set in. And I would have liked to have known

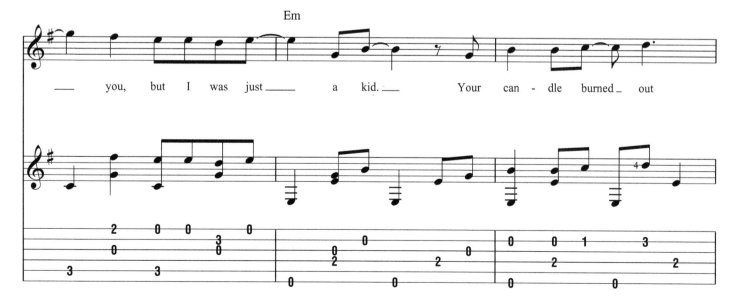

you, but I was just a kid. Your can-dle burned out

Additional lyrics

2. Loneliness was tough, the toughest role you ever played.
   Hollywood created a superstar and pain was the price you paid.
   And even when you died, oh, the press still hounded you.
   All the papers had to say was that Marilyn was found in the nude.

3. Goodbye, Norma Jean. Though I never knew you at all,
   You had the grace to hold yourself while those around you crawled.
   Goodbye, Norma Jean, from a young man in the twenty-second row,
   Who sees you as something more than sexual, more than just our Marilyn Monroe.

Don't Go Breaking My Heart

Words and Music by Carte Blanche and Ann Orson

Intro
Moderately

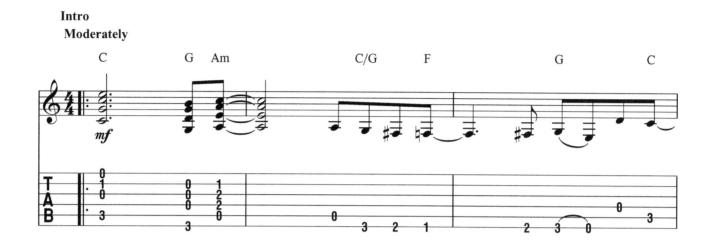

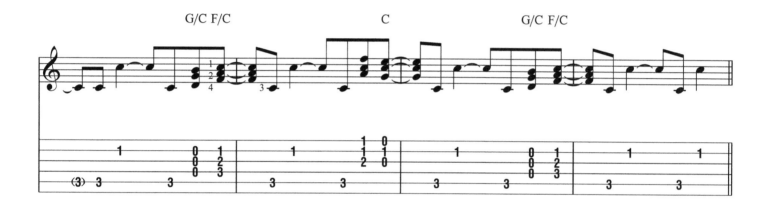

Verse

1. Don't go break-ing my heart. ___ I could-n't if I tried. ___
2. And no-bod-y told ___ us, 'cause no-bod-y showed ___

Copyright © 1976 HST MGT. LTD. and ROUGE BOOZE, INC.
Copyright Renewed
This arrangement Copyright © 2018 HST MGT. LTD. and ROUGE BOOZE, INC.
All Rights for HST MGT. LTD. in the United States and Canada Controlled and Administered by
UNIVERSAL - SONGS OF POLYGRAM INTERNATIONAL, INC.
All Rights for ROUGE BOOZE, INC. in the United States and Canada Controlled and Administered by
UNIVERSAL - POLYGRAM INTERNATIONAL PUBLISHING, INC.
All Rights Reserved   Used by Permission

Oh, hon - ey, if I _____ get rest - less.
_____ us. And now _____ it's up _____ to us, _____ babe.

Ba - by, you're not that kind. _____
Whoa, I think we can make _____ it.

Don't go break - ing my heart. _____
So don't mis - un - der - stand _____ me.

You take the weight off of me. _____
You put the light in my life. _____

Oh, hon - ey, when you knock on my door... __
Oh, you put the spark __ to the flame. __

Ooh, I gave you my key. __
I got your heart in my sights. __

Pre-Chorus

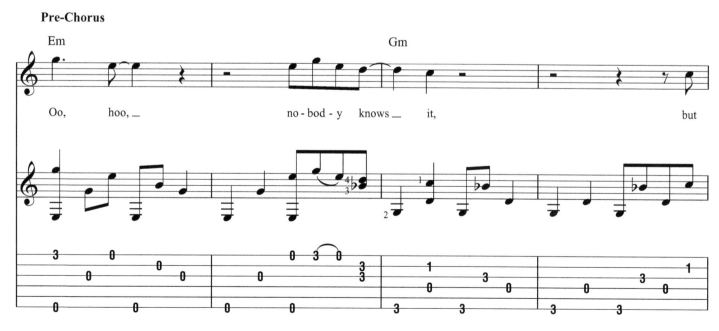

Oo, hoo, __ no - bod - y knows __ it, but

when I was down, _____ I was your clown. _____ Oo, hoo, ___

no - bod - y knows ___ it, no - bod - y knows _____ it, but

right from the start, _____ I gave you my heart. _____ Oh, _____ oh, __

I gave you my heart.

Chorus

So don't go break-ing my heart. I won't go break-ing your heart.

Don't go break-ing my heart.

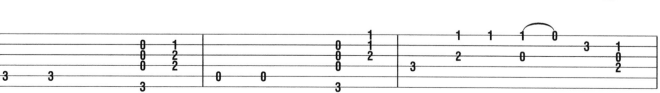

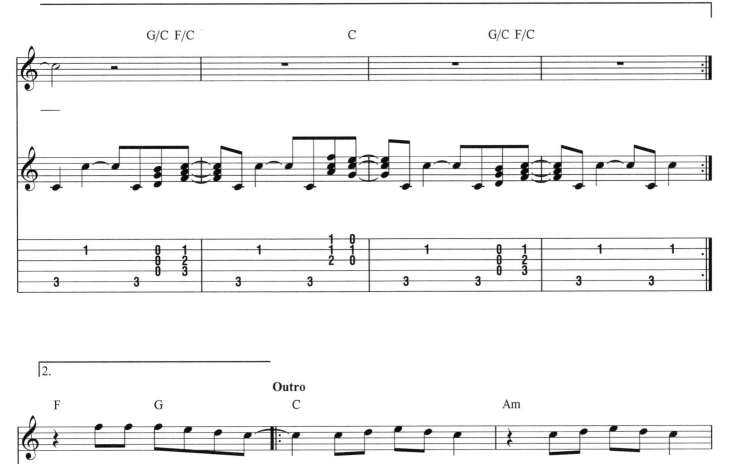

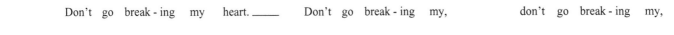

Daniel

Words and Music by Elton John and Bernie Taupin

Intro
Moderately fast

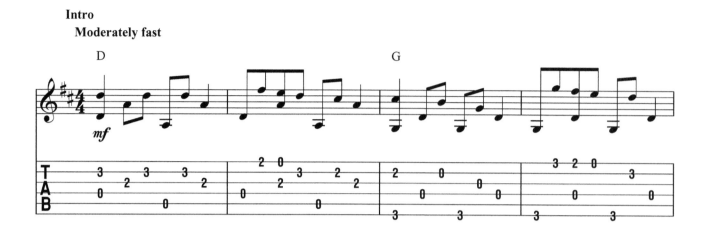

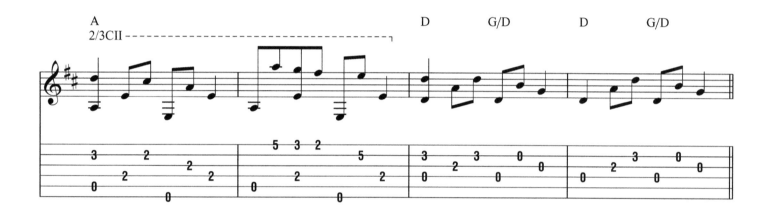

1., 3. Dan - iel is trav - 'ling to - night___ on a plane.___
2. They say Spain is pret - ty. No, I've nev - er been.

Copyright © 1972 UNIVERSAL/DICK JAMES MUSIC LTD.
Copyright Renewed
This arrangement Copyright © 2018 UNIVERSAL/DICK JAMES MUSIC LTD.
All Rights in the United States and Canada Controlled and Administered by UNIVERSAL - SONGS OF POLYGRAM INTERNATIONAL, INC.
All Rights Reserved   Used by Permission

I can see the red ___ tail - lights ___ head - ing for Spain, ___
Well, Dan - iel says ___ it's the best ___ place he's ev - ___ er seen, ___

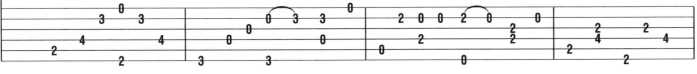

___ oh, ___ and I can see Dan - iel ___ wav - ing good - bye. ___
___ oh, ___ and he should know. ___ He's been ___ there e - nough. ___

God, it looks ___ like Dan - iel, must ___ be the clouds ___
Lord, I ___ miss Dan - iel, oh, ___ I miss ___

1.

To Coda

G/A   D

in ___ my eyes. ___
him ___ so ___

2.

A   D

much.   Oh, ___

Bridge

G   D

Dan - iel, ___ my broth - er, you are old - er ___ than ___ me. ___ Do you ___ still

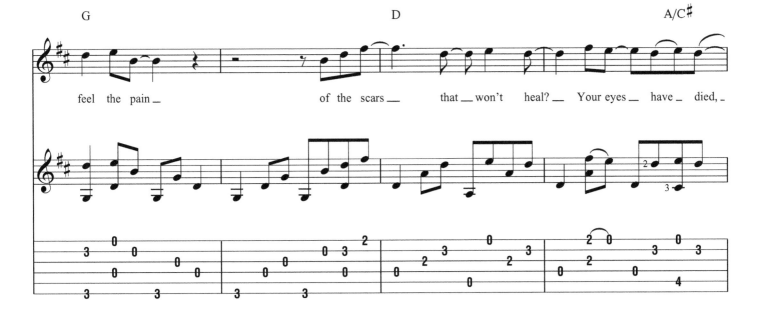

feel the pain ___ of the scars ___ that ___ won't heal? ___ Your eyes ___ have ___ died, ___

___ but you see more ___ than ___ I. ___ Dan - iel, you're a

D.S. al Coda

star in the face ___ of the sky. ___

Coda

Oh, God, __ it _____ looks like Dan - iel,

must be ___ the clouds ___ in ___ my eyes. ___

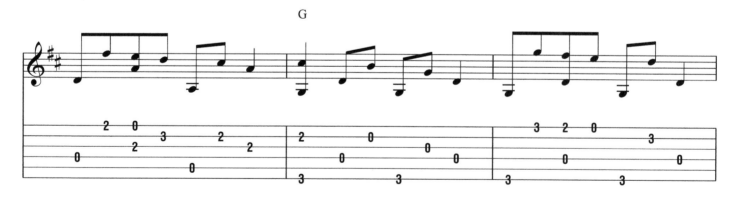

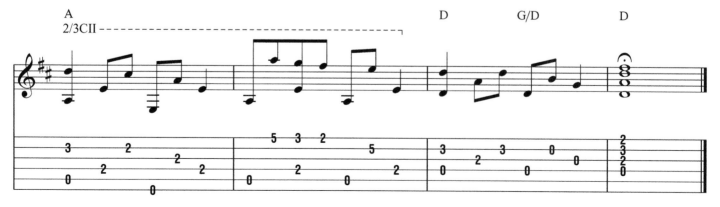

Don't Let the Sun Go Down on Me

Words and Music by Elton John and Bernie Taupin

Drop D tuning:
(low to high) D-A-D-G-B-E

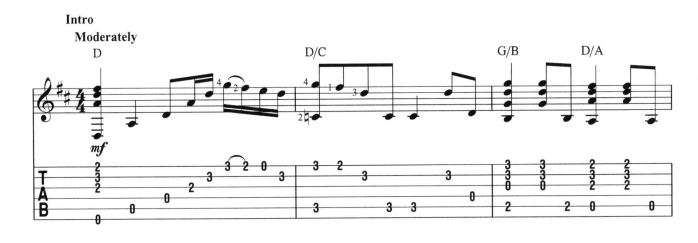

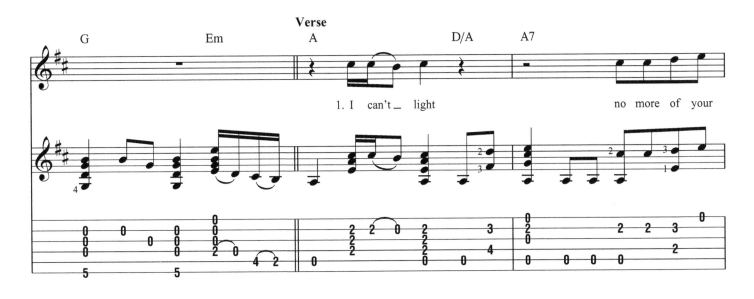

Copyright © 1974 HST MGT. LTD. and ROUGE BOOZE, INC.
Copyright Renewed
This arrangement Copyright © 2018 HST MGT. LTD. and ROUGE BOOZE, INC.
All Rights for HST MGT. LTD. in the United States and Canada Controlled and Administered by
UNIVERSAL - SONGS OF POLYGRAM INTERNATIONAL, INC.
All Rights for ROUGE BOOZE, INC. in the United States and Canada Controlled and Administered by
UNIVERSAL - POLYGRAM INTERNATIONAL PUBLISHING, INC.
All Rights Reserved   Used by Permission

seem to fade to black and white.

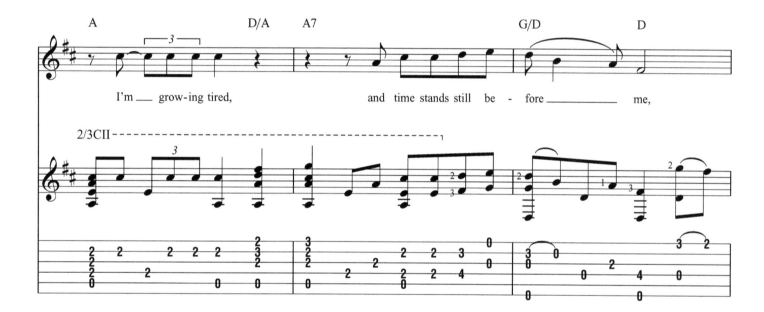

I'm ___ grow-ing tired, and time stands still be - fore ___ me,

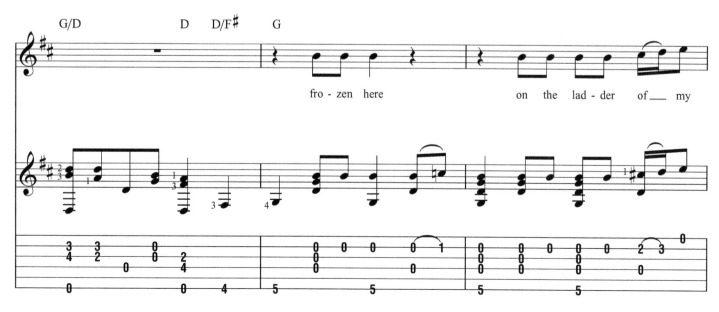

fro - zen here on the lad - der of ___ my

life. Too late ___

to save my-self from fall - ing.

I ___ took a chance and changed your way of life.

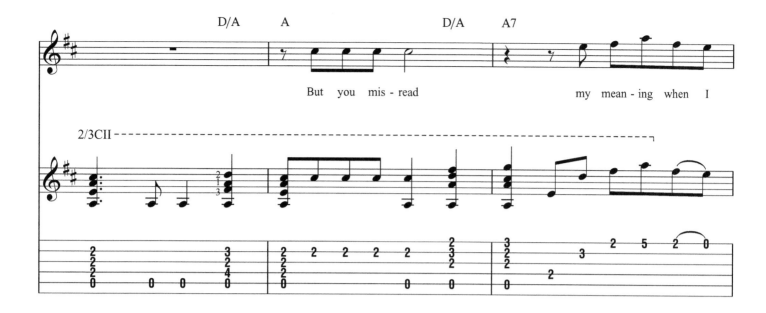

But you mis-read my mean-ing when I

met you. Closed the door

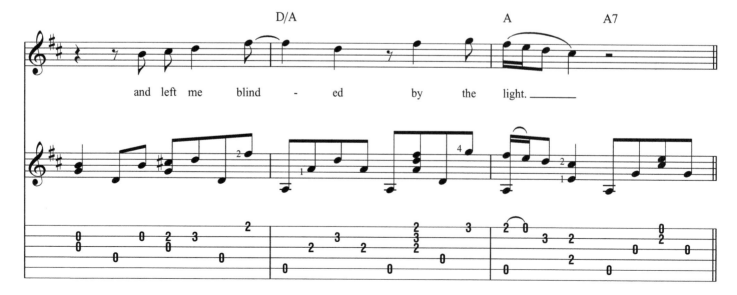

and left me blind-ed by the light.

𝄋 Chorus

Don't let the sun _____ go down on me. _____ Al-though I search my-self, it's al-ways

some-one else I see. _____ I'd just al-low a frag-ment of your life _____ to wan-der

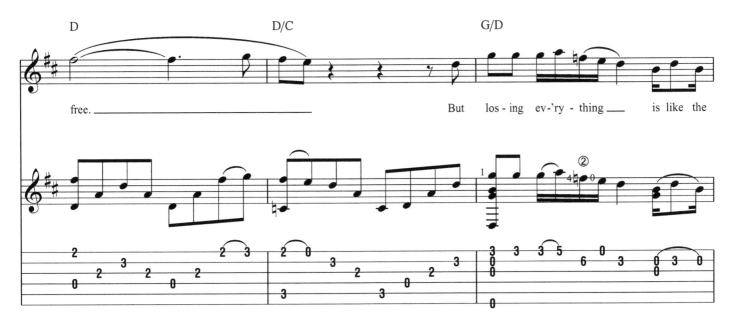

free. _____ But los-ing ev-'ry-thing _____ is like the

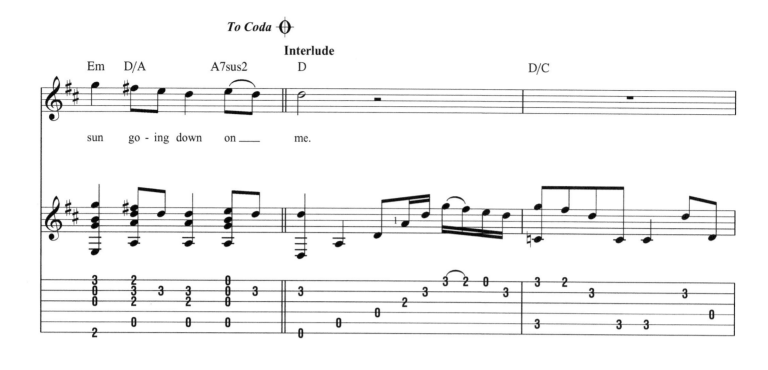

To Coda

Interlude

sun go - ing down on ___ me.

2. I can't find,

oh, ___ the right ro - man - tic ___ line.

But see me once and see the way I feel.

Don't dis-card me just be-cause you

think I mean you harm. But these cuts I have,

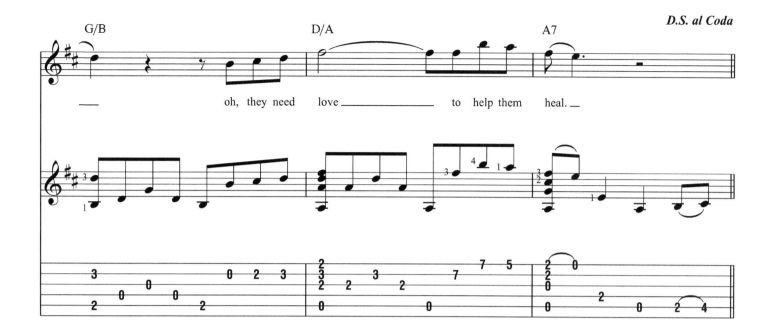

oh, they need love _____ to help them heal. _

Coda

Outro

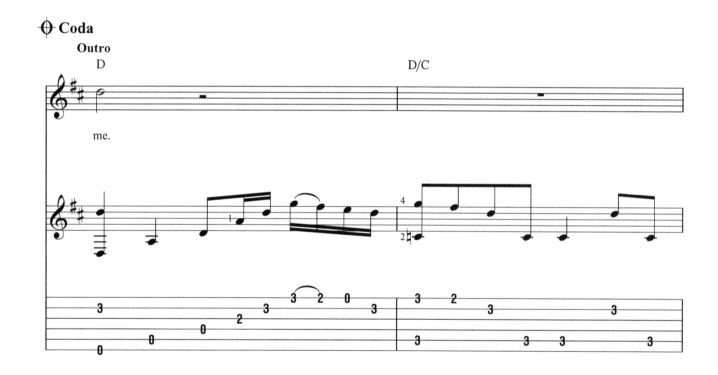

me.

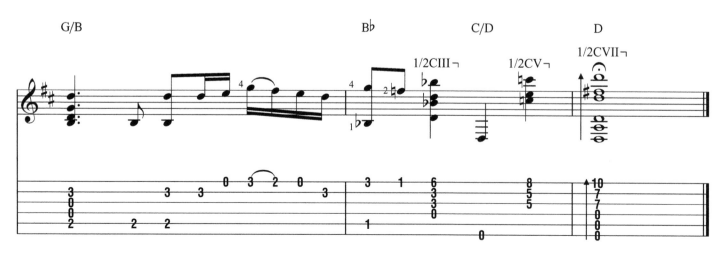

Goodbye Yellow Brick Road

Words and Music by Elton John and Bernie Taupin

1. When are you gon-na come down? When are you go-ing to land?
2. What do you think you'll do then? I bet that-'ll shoot down your plane.

I should have stayed on the farm, should have lis-
It-'ll take you a cou-ple of vod-ka and ton-ics to

Copyright © 1973 UNIVERSAL/DICK JAMES MUSIC LTD.
Copyright Renewed
This arrangement Copyright © 2018 UNIVERSAL/DICK JAMES MUSIC LTD.
All Rights in the United States and Canada Controlled and Administered by UNIVERSAL - SONGS OF POLYGRAM INTERNATIONAL, INC.
All Rights Reserved   Used by Permission

tened to my old man.
set you on your feet a - gain.
You know you can't hold me for - ev -
May - be you'll get a re - place -

- er.
- ment,
I did - n't sign up with you.
there's plen - ty like me to be found.
I'm

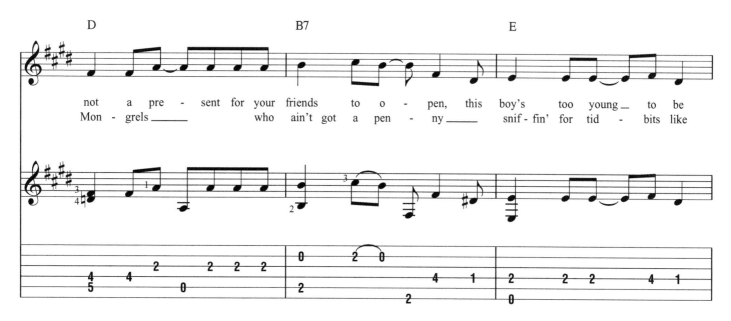

not a pre - sent for your friends to o - pen, this boy's too young to be
Mon - grels who ain't got a pen - ny snif - fin' for tid - bits like

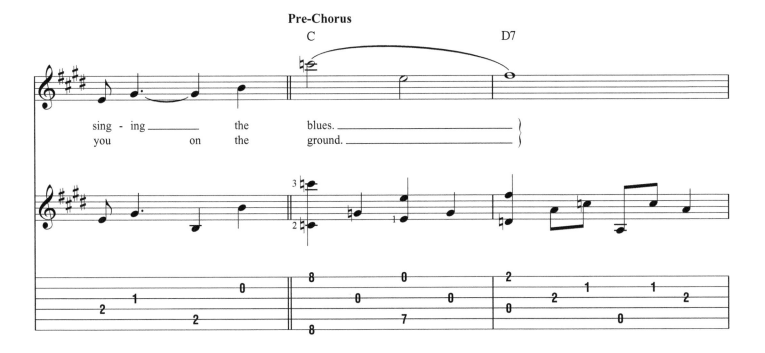

Pre-Chorus

sing - ing _____ the blues. _____
you on the ground. _____

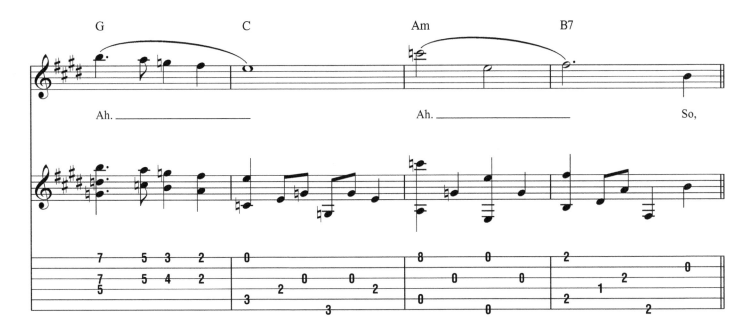

Ah. _____   Ah. _____   So,

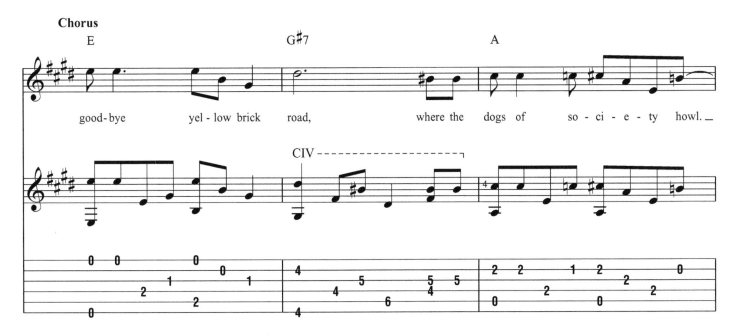

Chorus

good - bye yel - low brick road, where the dogs of so - ci - e - ty howl. _

You can't plant me in your pent - house, _____ I'm

go - ing back _ to my plough. Back to the howl - ing old owl _

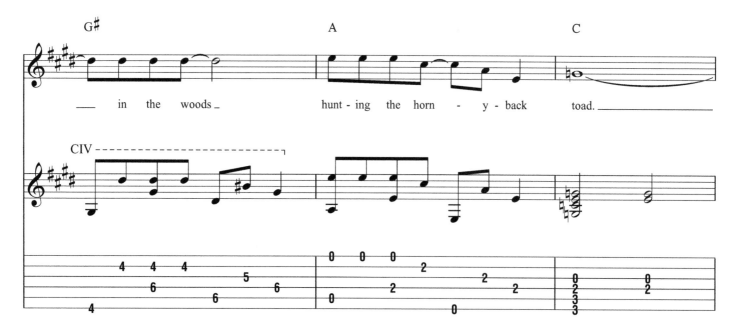

_ in the woods _ hunt - ing the horn - y - back toad. _____

Oh, I've fi - n'lly de - cid - ed my fu - ture lies ___ be -

yond the yel - low brick road. ___ Ah. ___

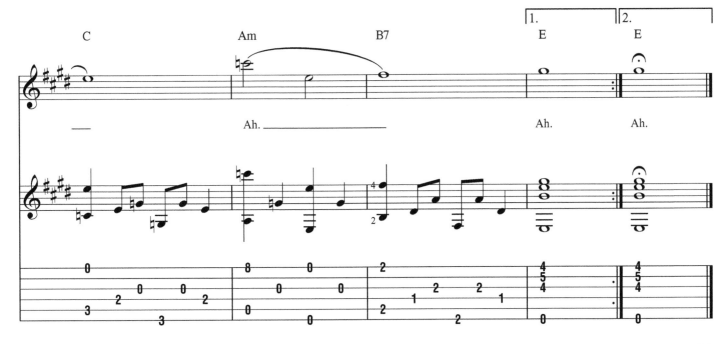

___ Ah. ___ Ah. Ah.

I Guess That's Why They Call It the Blues

Words and Music by Elton John, Bernie Taupin and Davey Johnstone

1. Don't wish it a - way. Don't look at it like it's for - ever.
2. Just stare in - to space, pic - ture my face in your hands.

Be - tween you and me,
Live for each sec -

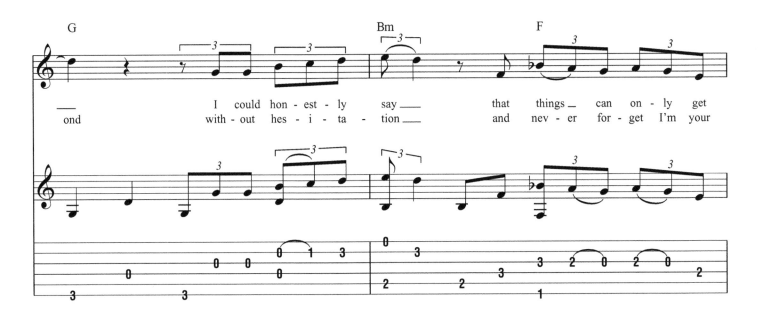

I could hon - est - ly say ___ that things ___ can on - ly get
ond with - out hes - i - ta - tion ___ and nev - er for - get I'm your

bet - ter. And while I'm ___ a - way, ___
man. ___ Wait on ___ me girl. ___

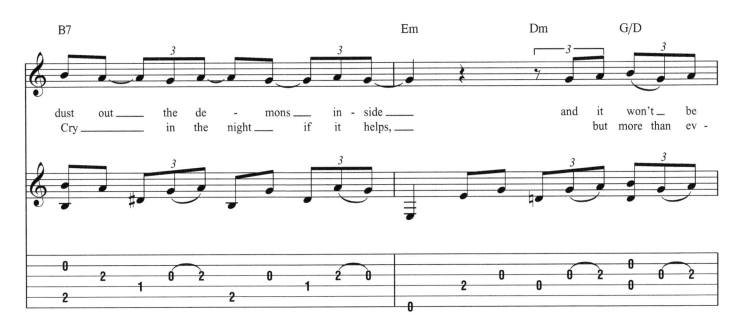

dust out ___ the de - mons ___ in - side ___ and it won't ___ be
Cry ___ in the night ___ if it helps, ___ but more than ev -

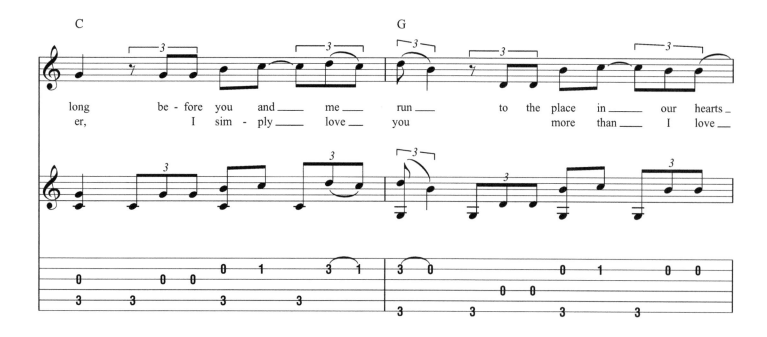

long be-fore you and me run to the place in our hearts
er, I sim-ply love you more than I love

where we hide.
life it-self.

And I

Chorus

guess that's why they call it the blues. Time on my

hands could be time spent with you laugh - ing like child - ren, liv - ing like

lov - ers, roll - ing like thun - der, un - der the cov - ers. And I

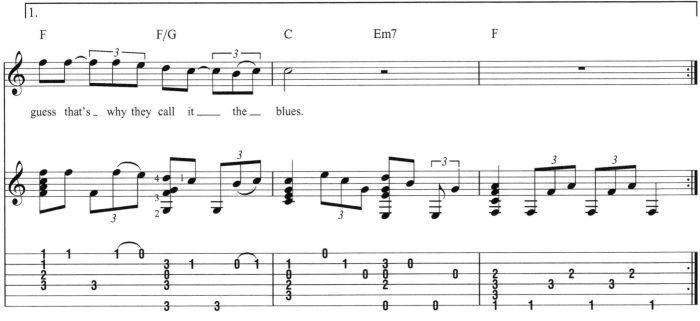

guess that's why they call it the blues.

guess that's ___ why they call it ___ the ___ blues. Laugh - ing like child - ren,

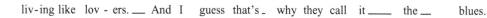

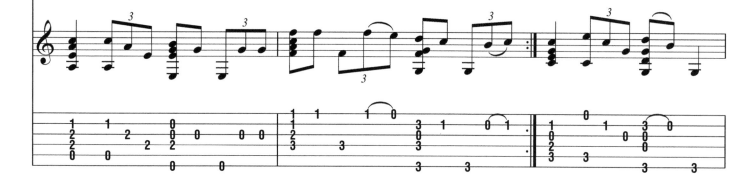

liv-ing like lov - ers. ___ And I guess that's ___ why they call it ___ the ___ blues.

And I guess that's ___ why they call it ___ the ___ blues.

Mona Lisas and Mad Hatters

Words and Music by Elton John and Bernie Taupin

Verse
Slow

1. And now I know "Span - ish Har -
2. This Broad - way's got, it's got a lot of songs

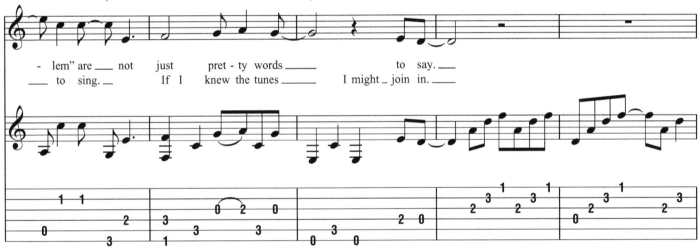

- lem" are not just pret - ty words to say.
to sing. If I knew the tunes I might join in.

I thought I knew, but now I know that rose trees
I go my way a - lone, grow my own. My own seeds

Copyright © 1972 UNIVERSAL/DICK JAMES MUSIC LTD.
Copyright Renewed
This arrangement Copyright © 2018 UNIVERSAL/DICK JAMES MUSIC LTD.
All Rights in the United States and Canada Controlled and Administered by UNIVERSAL - SONGS OF POLYGRAM INTERNATIONAL, INC.
All Rights Reserved   Used by Permission

nev - er grow / shall be sown   in New York Cit - y.

Un - til you seen this trash - can dream come true, / Sub - way's no way for a good man to go down.

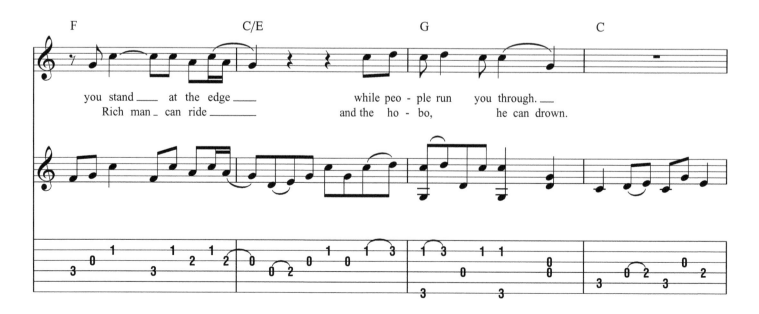

you stand at the edge while peo - ple run you through. / Rich man can ride and the ho - bo, he can drown.

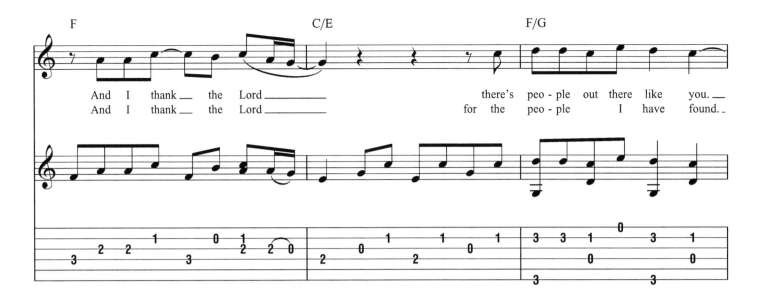

And I thank __ the Lord _____ there's peo-ple out there like you. __
And I thank __ the Lord _____ for the peo-ple I have found. __

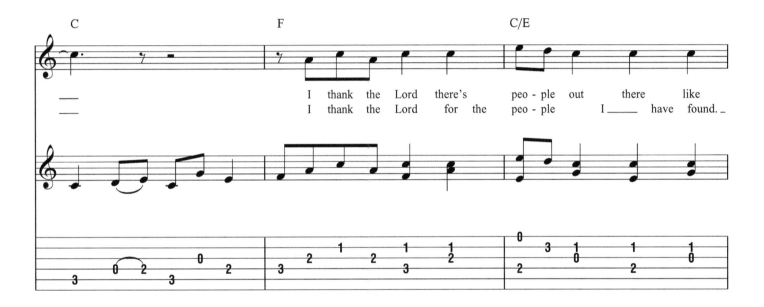

I thank the Lord there's peo-ple out there like
I thank the Lord for the peo-ple I __ have found. __

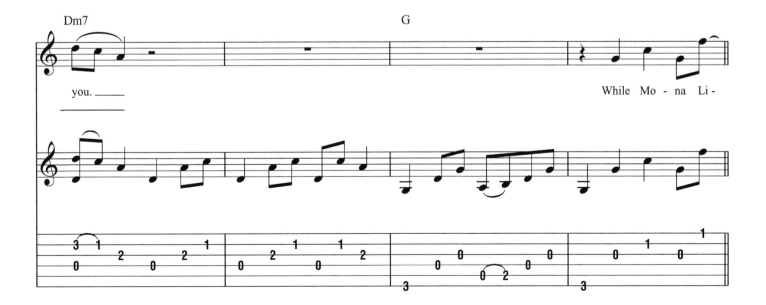

you. ____ While Mo - na Li -

Chorus

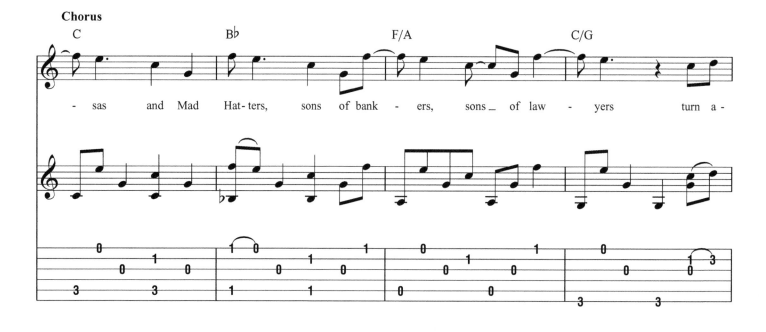

-sas and Mad Hat- ters, sons of bank - ers, sons of law - yers turn a-

round and say, "Good morn - ing" to the night. For un-

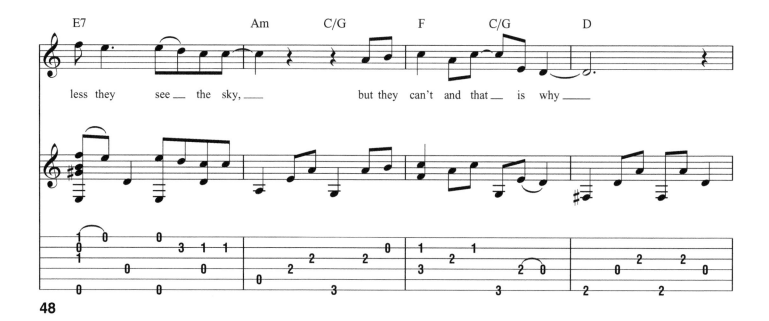

less they see the sky, but they can't and that is why

they know not if ____ it's dark ____ out - side ____ or light.

They know not if ____ it's dark ____

out - side ____ or light.

Levon

Words and Music by Elton John and Bernie Taupin

*Hold low C note, next 12 meas.

1. Le - von wears his war __ wounds like a crown. __
2. Le - von sells car - toon __ bal - loons in town. __

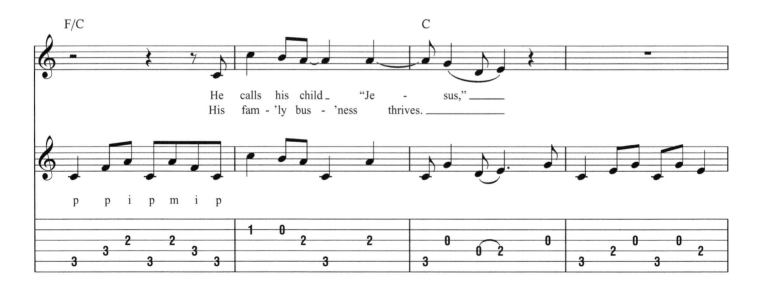

He calls his child __ "Je - sus," _____
His fam - 'ly bus - 'ness thrives. _____

'cause he likes the name ___ and he
Je - sus blows up ___ bal - loons all day, ___ sits on ___

sends him to ___ the fin - est schools ___ in town. ___
___ the porch ___ swing, watch - ing ___ them fly. ___ And

Le - von, Le - von likes his mon - ey. ___
Je - sus, he wants ___ to go ___ to Ve - nus, ___

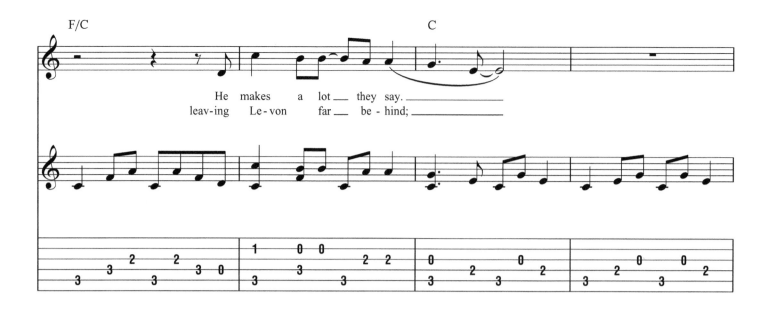

He makes a lot they say.
leav-ing Le-von far be-hind;

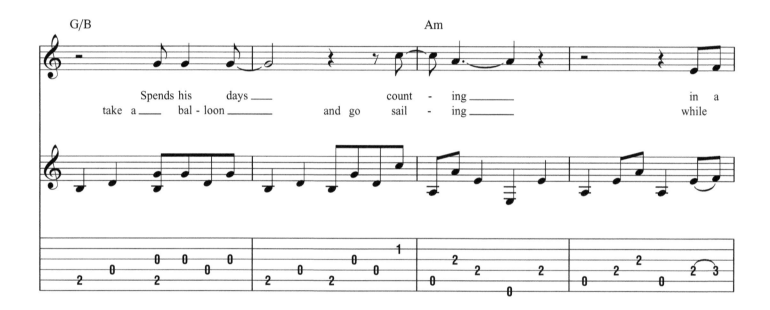

Spends his days count - ing in a
take a bal-loon and go sail - ing while

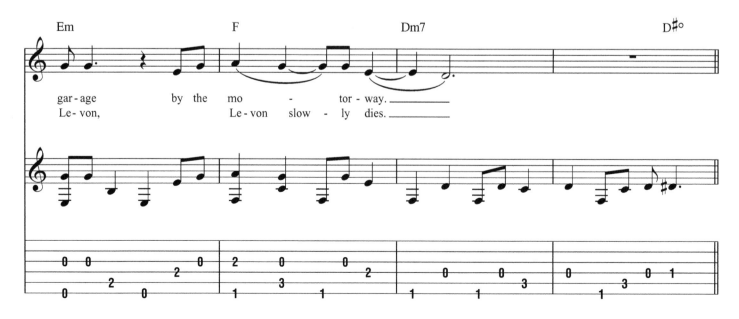

gar-age by the mo - tor-way.
Le-von, Le-von slow-ly dies.

Pre-Chorus

He was born a pau - per to a pawn on a Christ-mas day, when the New York Times said God

is dead, and the war's be - gun. Al - vin Tos - tig has a son to - day.

And he shall be Le -

Chorus

- von. __ And he shall __ be a good __ man. __

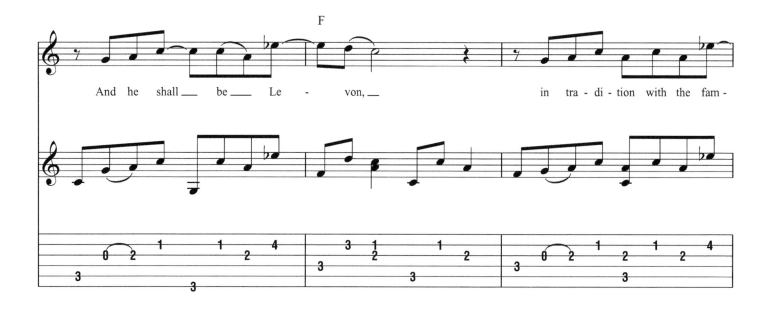

And he shall __ be __ Le - von, __ in tra - di - tion with the fam-

- 'ly plan. __ And he shall __ be __ Le - von. __

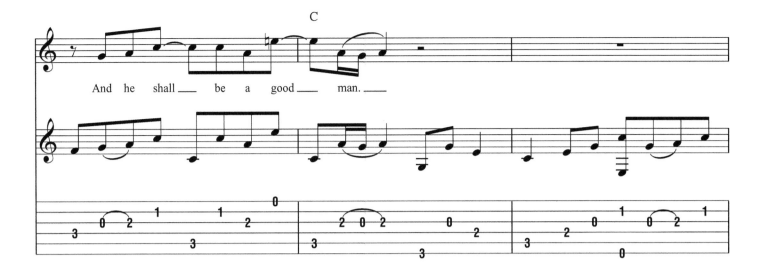

And he shall___ be a good___ man.___

He shall___ be___ Le - von.___

Outro

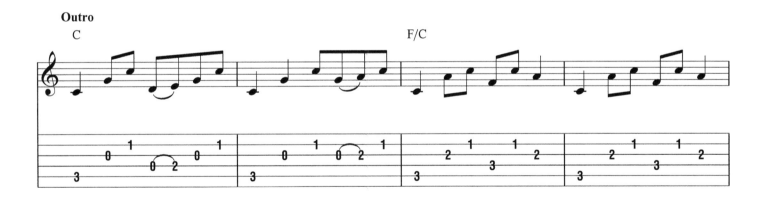

Rocket Man
(I Think It's Gonna Be a Long Long Time)
Words and Music by Elton John and Bernie Taupin

1. She packed my bags last night, pre-flight,
2. Mars ain't the kind of place to raise your kids.

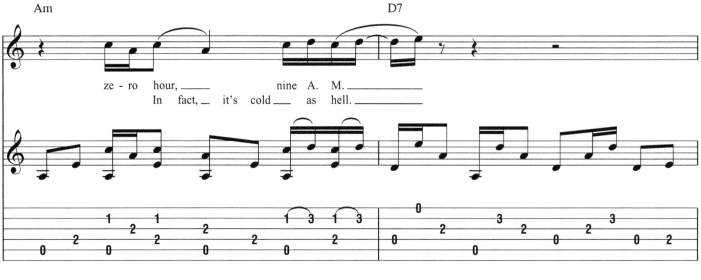

ze-ro hour, nine A. M.
In fact, it's cold as hell.

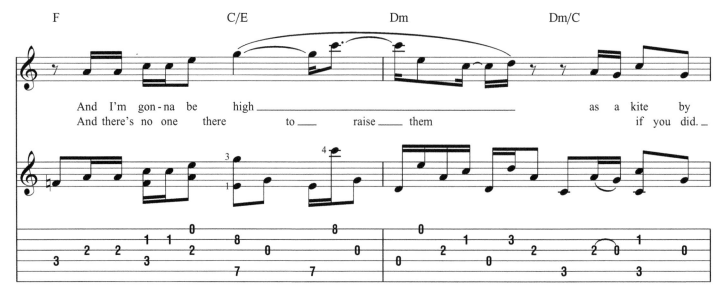

And I'm gon-na be high as a kite by
And there's no one there to raise them if you did.

Copyright © 1972 UNIVERSAL/DICK JAMES MUSIC LTD.
Copyright Renewed
This arrangement Copyright © 2018 UNIVERSAL/DICK JAMES MUSIC LTD.
All Rights in the United States and Canada Controlled and Administered by UNIVERSAL - SONGS OF POLYGRAM INTERNATIONAL, INC.
All Rights Reserved   Used by Permission

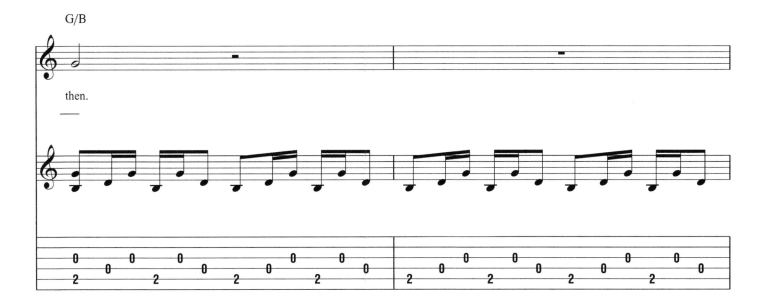

then.

I miss__ the earth__ so much, I miss my wife.
And all__ this sci-ence I don't un - der - stand.

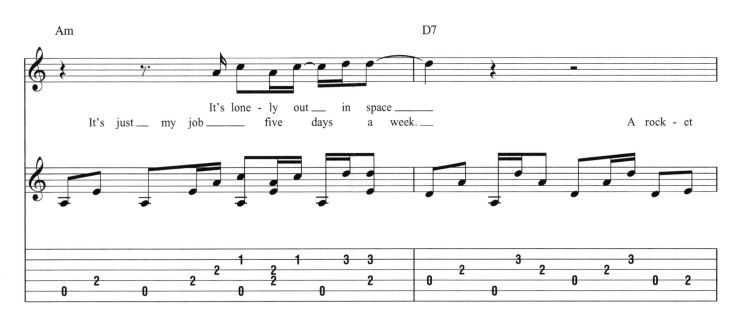

It's lone - ly out__ in space_____
It's just__ my job_____ five days a week.__ A rock - et

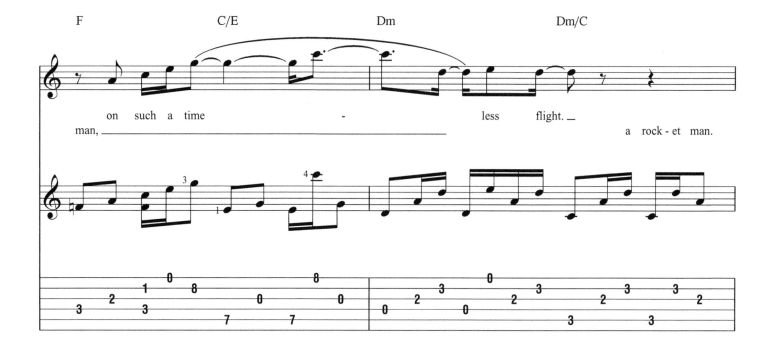

on such a time - less flight. _

man, _____ a rock - et man.

Chorus

And I think it's gon-na be a long, _ long time till touch - down brings _ me 'round a-gain to find

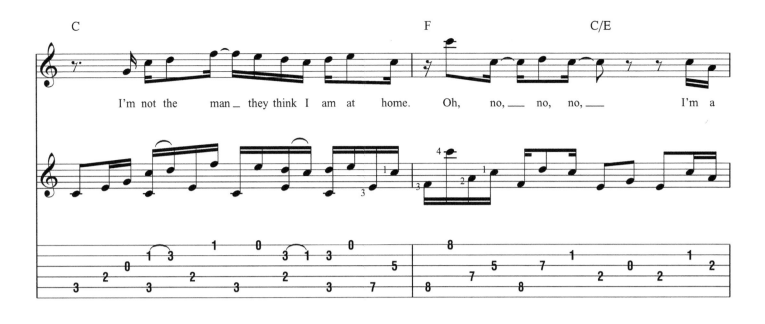

I'm not the man _ they think I am at home. Oh, no, __ no, no, __ I'm a

rock - et man. _____ Rock - et man, _ burn - ing out his fuse up here _

_ a - lone.

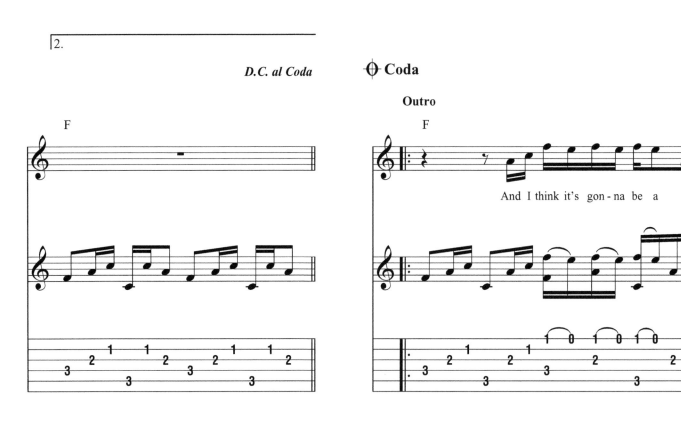

D.C. al Coda   **Coda**

Outro

And I think it's gon-na be a   long, _

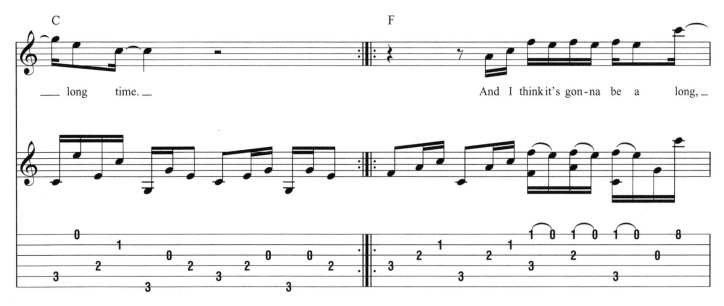

_ long   time. _

And I think it's gon-na be a   long, _

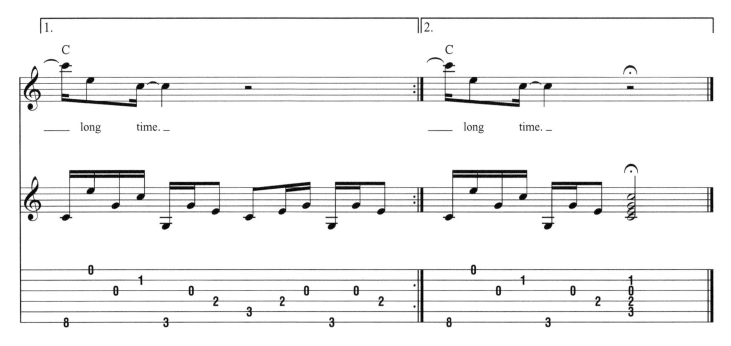

_ long   time. _

_ long   time. _

Someone Saved My Life Tonight

Words and Music by Elton John and Bernie Taupin

Intro
Slow

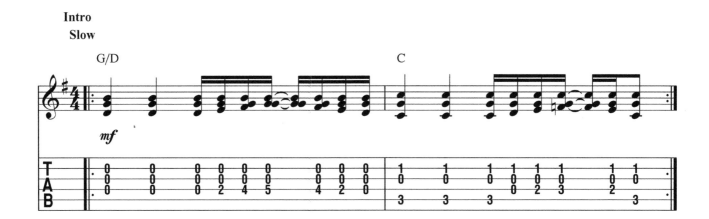

Verse

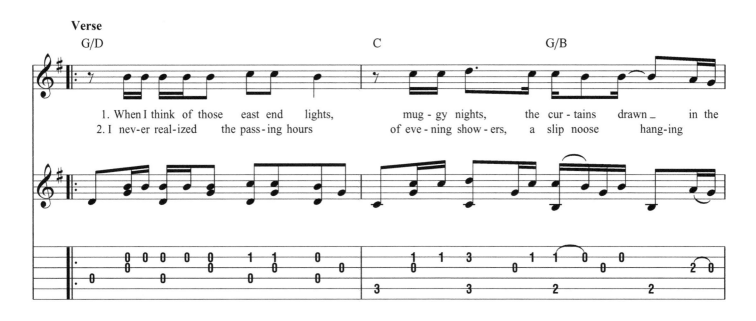

1. When I think of those east end lights, mug-gy nights, the cur-tains drawn _ in the
2. I nev-er real-ized the pass-ing hours of eve-ning show-ers, a slip noose hang-ing

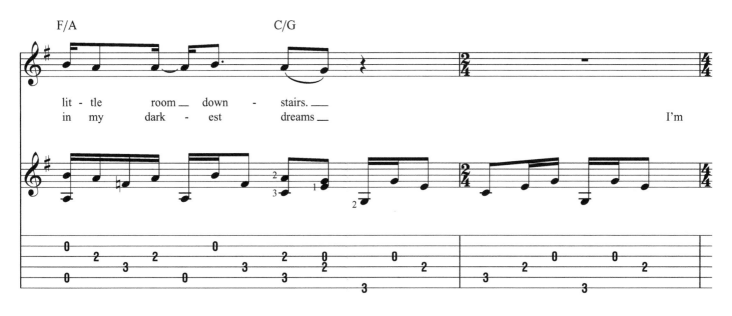

lit-tle room _ down - stairs. _
in my dark-est dreams _   I'm

Copyright © 1975 HST MGT. LTD. and ROUGE BOOZE, INC.
Copyright Renewed
This arrangement Copyright © 2018 HST MGT. LTD. and ROUGE BOOZE, INC.
All Rights for HST MGT. LTD. in the United States and Canada Controlled and Administered by
UNIVERSAL - SONGS OF POLYGRAM INTERNATIONAL, INC.
All Rights for ROUGE BOOZE, INC. in the United States and Canada Controlled and Administered by
UNIVERSAL - POLYGRAM INTERNATIONAL PUBLISHING, INC.
All Rights Reserved   Used by Permission

Pri - ma don - na, Lord, you real - ly should have been there
stran - gled by your haunt - ed so - cial scene,

sit - ting like a prin - cess perched in her e - lec - tric chair. And it's
just a pawn out - played by a dom - i - nat - ing queen. It's

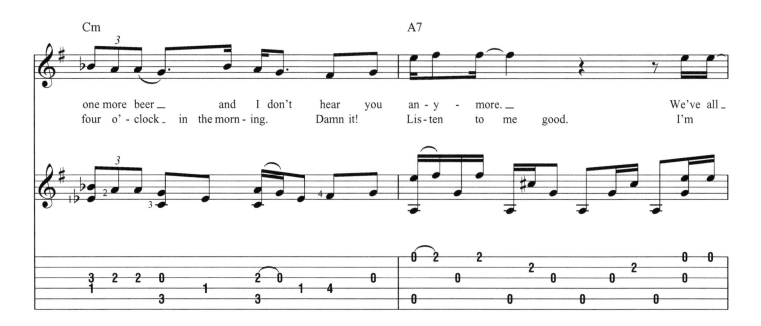

one more beer and I don't hear you an - y - more. We've all
four o' - clock in the morn - ing. Damn it! Lis - ten to me good. I'm

gone cra - zy late - ly, my friends out there __ roll - in' 'round __ the base-
sleep - ing with my - self __ to night, saved in time. __ Thank God my mu - sic's still

- ment floor. _
a - live.

𝄋 Chorus

And some - one __ saved my life to - night, _ su - gar bear.

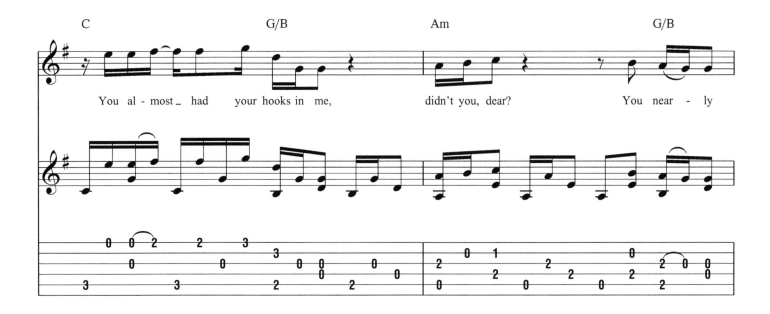

You al-most_ had your hooks in me, didn't you, dear? You near-ly

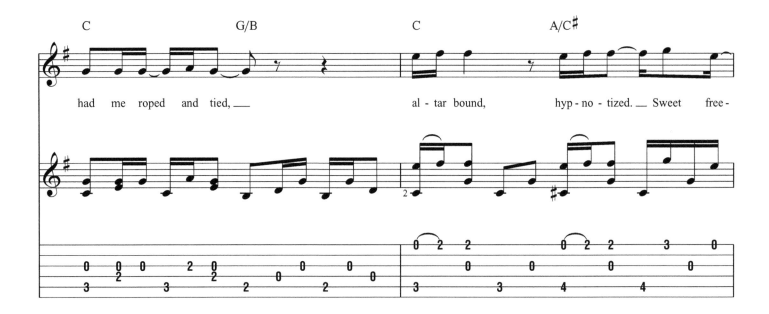

had me roped and tied, _ al-tar bound, hyp-no-tized. _ Sweet free-

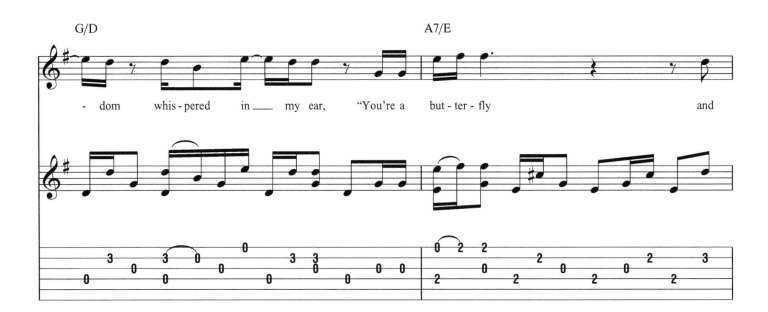

-dom whis-pered in __ my ear, "You're a but-ter-fly and

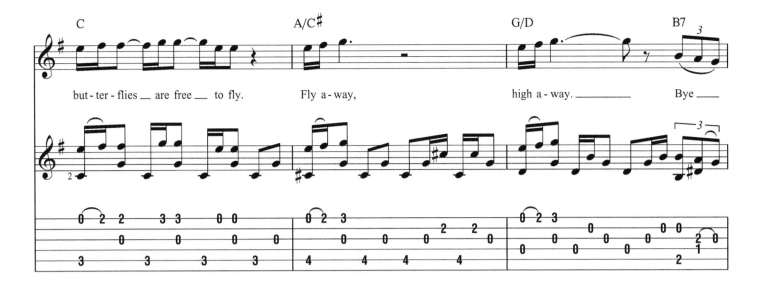

but - ter - flies __ are free __ to fly. Fly a - way, high a - way. _____ Bye __

bye." Oh. _____

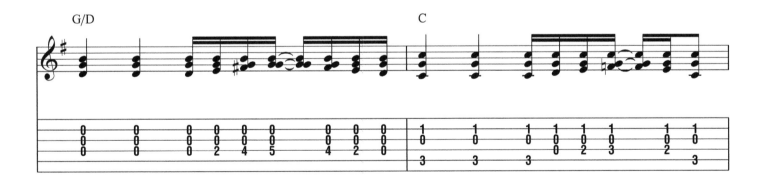

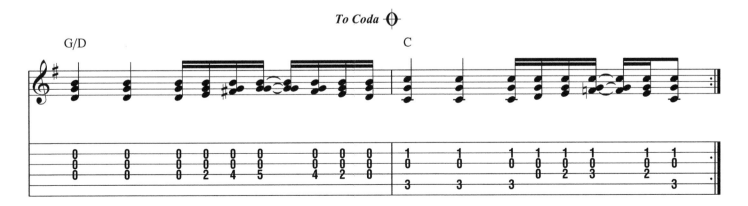

To Coda

Bridge

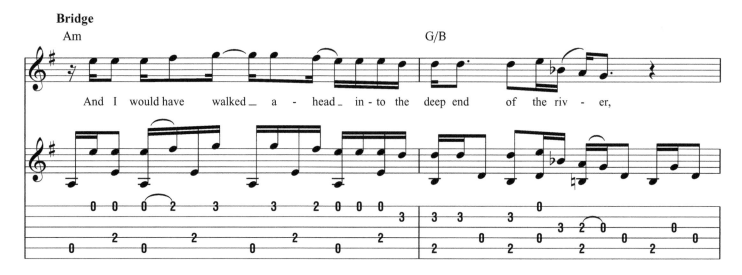

And I would have walked _ a - head _ in - to the deep end of the riv - er,

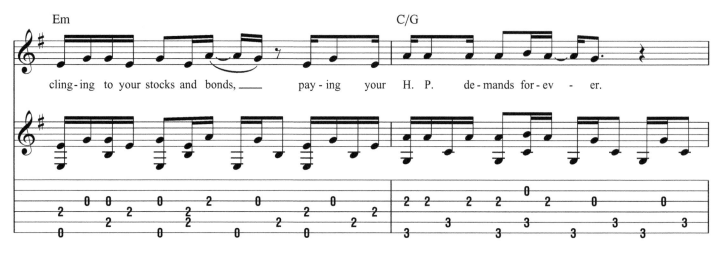

cling-ing to your stocks and bonds, ___ pay - ing your H. P. de - mands for - ev - er.

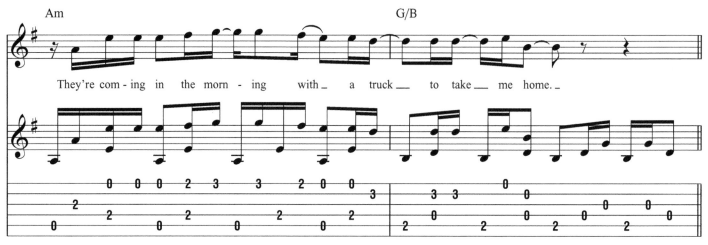

They're com - ing in the morn - ing with _ a truck _ to take _ me home. _

Some - one saved my life _ to - night. Some - one saved my life _ to - night. ___

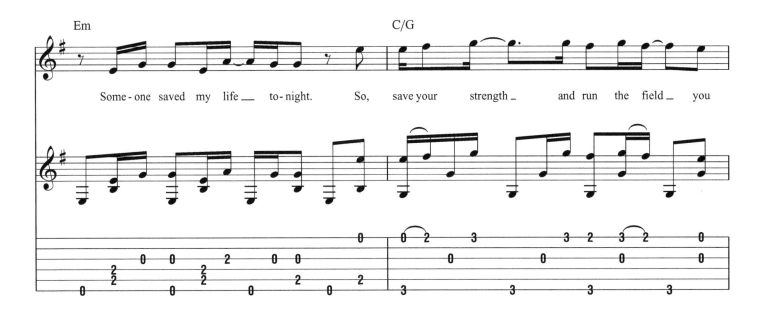

Some-one saved my life __ to-night. So, save your strength __ and run the field __ you

D.S. al Coda

Coda

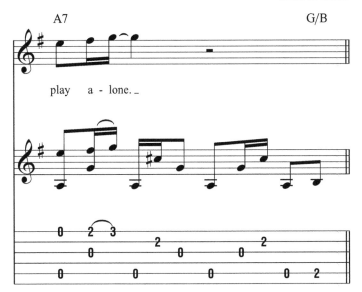

play a - lone. __

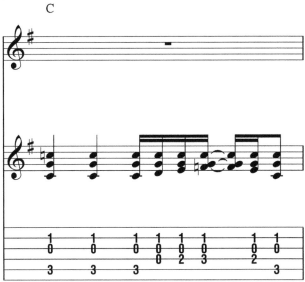

Outro

Some-one saved, some-one saved, some-one saved my life __ to-night. __

Something About the Way You Look Tonight

Words and Music by Elton John and Bernie Taupin

Copyright © 1997 WAB MANAGEMENT LIMITED and ROUGE BOOZE, INC.
This arrangement Copyright © 2018 WAB MANAGEMENT LIMITED and ROUGE BOOZE, INC.
All Rights for WAB MANAGEMENT LIMITED in the United States and Canada Controlled and Administered by
UNIVERSAL - SONGS OF POLYGRAM INTERNATIONAL, INC.
All Rights for ROUGE BOOZE, INC. in the United States and Canada Controlled and Administered by
UNIVERSAL - POLYGRAM INTERNATIONAL PUBLISHING, INC.
All Rights Reserved   Used by Permission

Verse

sun. _ 2. I need to tell _ you how you
smile _ you

light up ev - 'ry sec - ond of the day. _____
pull the deep - est se - crets from my heart. _

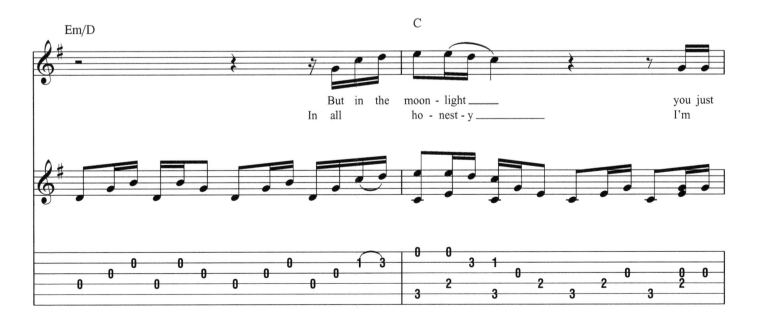

But in the moon - light _____ you just
In all ho - nest - y _____ I'm

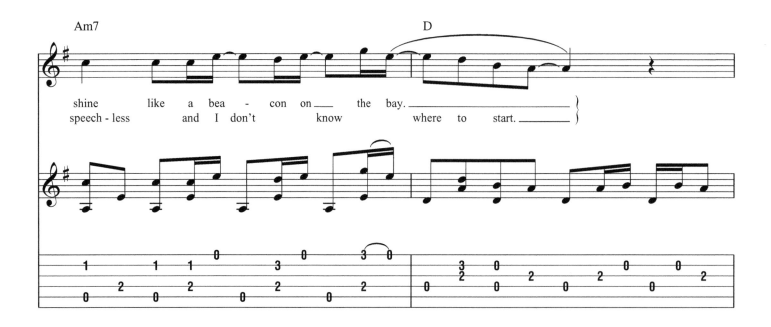

shine like a bea - con on the bay.
speech - less and I don't know where to start.

Chorus

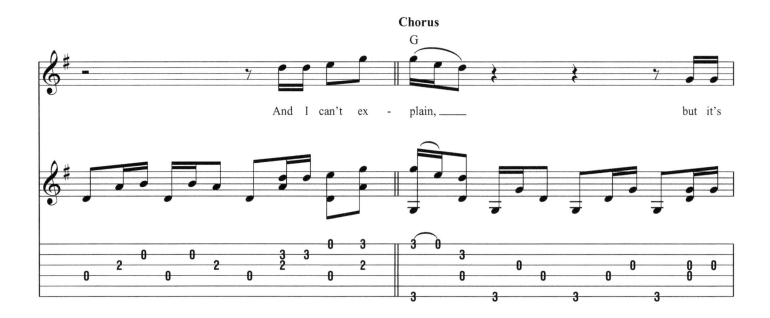

And I can't ex - plain, _____ but it's

some - thing a - bout the way the you look to - night.

Takes my breath a - way, _____ It's that

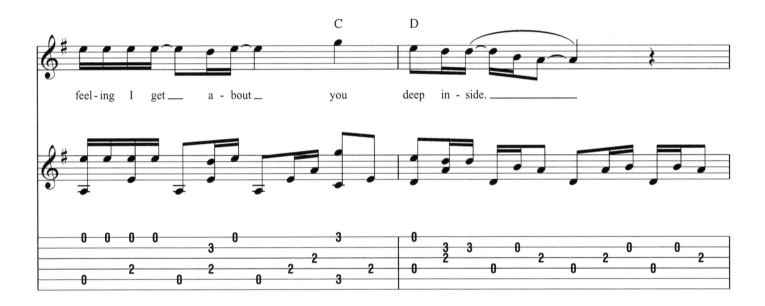

feel - ing I get __ a - bout __ you deep in - side. _____

And I can't de - scribe, ____ but it's

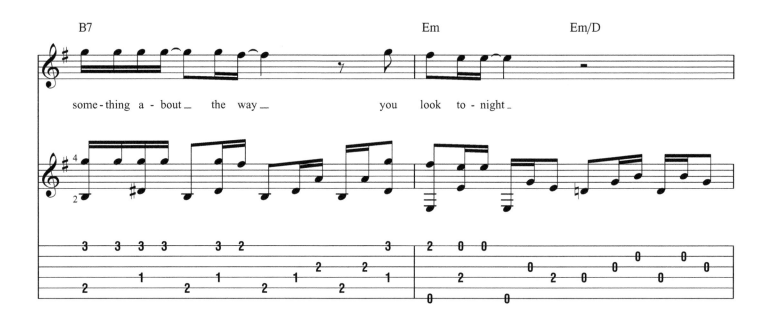

some-thing a - bout __ the way __ you look to - night __

takes my breath a - way. _____

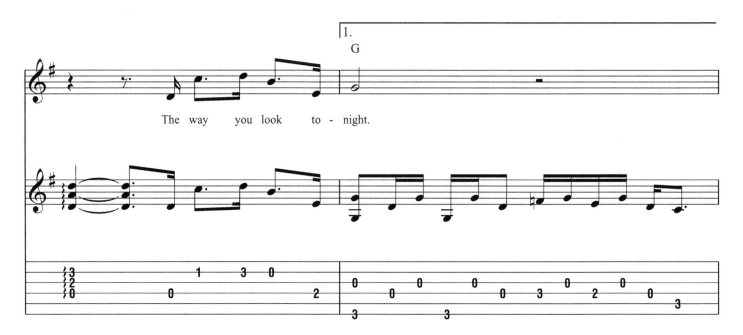

The way you look to - night.

3. With your night.

Outro

The way you look to - night. ___ The way you

look to - night. _____ The way you look to - night. _____

Your Song

Words and Music by Elton John and Bernie Taupin

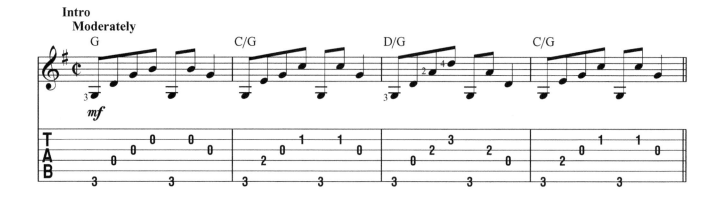

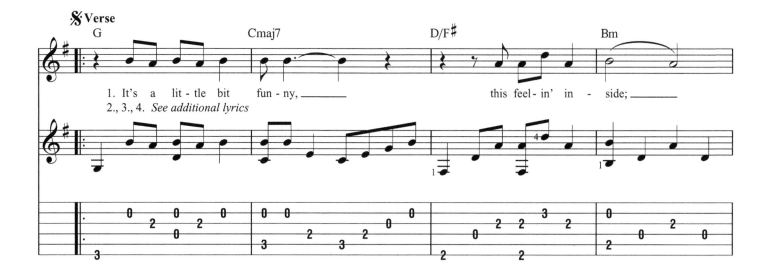

1. It's a lit-tle bit fun-ny, _____ this feel-in' in - side; _____
2., 3., 4. *See additional lyrics*

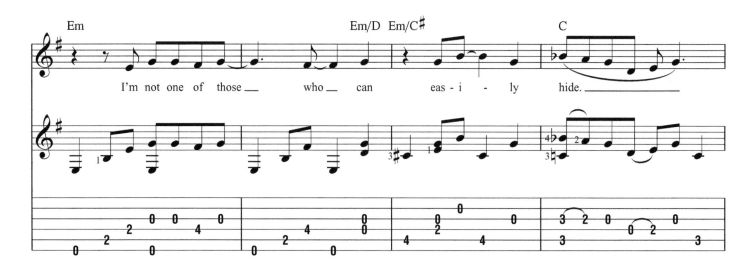

I'm not one of those _____ who _____ can eas-i - ly hide. _____

Copyright © 1969 UNIVERSAL/DICK JAMES MUSIC LTD.
Copyright Renewed
This arrangement Copyright © 2018 UNIVERSAL/DICK JAMES MUSIC LTD.
All Rights in the United States and Canada Controlled and Administered by UNIVERSAL - SONGS OF POLYGRAM INTERNATIONAL, INC.
All Rights Reserved   Used by Permission

Don't _ have much mon- ey, _____ but, boy, if I did, _____

I'd buy a big house where _____ we both could live.

___ this one's for you.

Chorus

And you can tell ev- 'ry- bod - y this is your song. _____

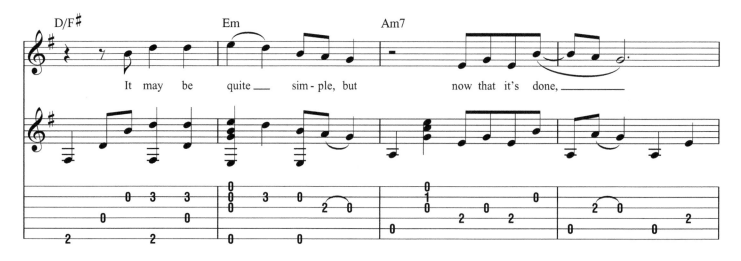

It may be quite ___ sim - ple, but now that it's done, ___

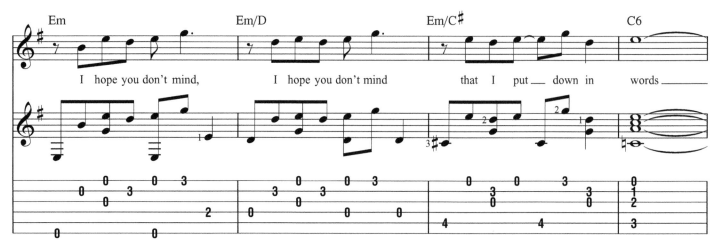

I hope you don't mind, I hope you don't mind that I put ___ down in words ___

___ how won - der - ful life is while you're ___ in ___ the world. ___

To Coda ⊕

D.S. al Coda
(take repeat)

⊕ Coda

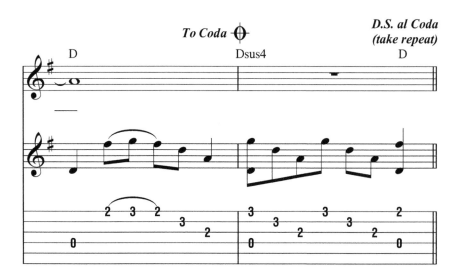

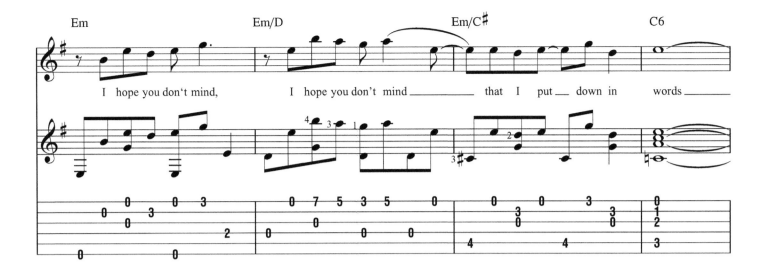

I hope you don't mind, I hope you don't mind _____ that I put ___ down in words _____

___ how won - der - ful life is while you're ___ in ___ the world. ___

Outro

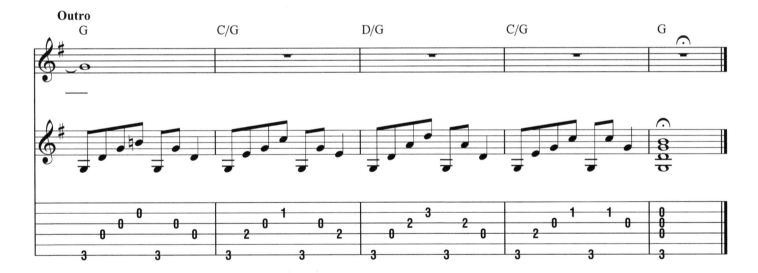

Additional Lyrics

2. If I was a sculptor, but then again, no.
   Or a man who makes potions in a traveling show.
   I know it's not much but it's the best I can do,
   My gift is my song and this one's for you.

3. I sat on the roof and kicked off the moss.
   Well, a few of the verses, well, they've got me quite cross,
   But the sun's been quite kind while I wrote this song.
   It's for people like you that keep it turned on.

4. So excuse me forgettin', but these things I do.
   You see, I've forgotten if they're green or they're blue.
   Anyway, the thing is what I really mean,
   Yours are the sweetest eyes I've ever seen.

Tiny Dancer

Words and Music by Elton John and Bernie Taupin

Intro

Slow

1., 3. Blue jean ba - by, L. A. la - dy,
2. Je - sus freaks out in the streets

Verse

seam - stress for the band.
hand - ing tick - ets out for God.

Pret - ty - eyed, _____ pi - rate smile, ___
Turn - ing back, ___ she _ just laughs. _

you'll mar - ry a mu - sic man. ___
The bou - le - vard ___ is not _ that bad. ___

Bal - le - ri - na, _____ you must __ have seen _____ her
Pia - no man, _____ he makes _ his stand ___

Dm/F   E7   Am   G/B

danc - ing in ___ the sand. ___
in the au - di - to - ri - um. ___

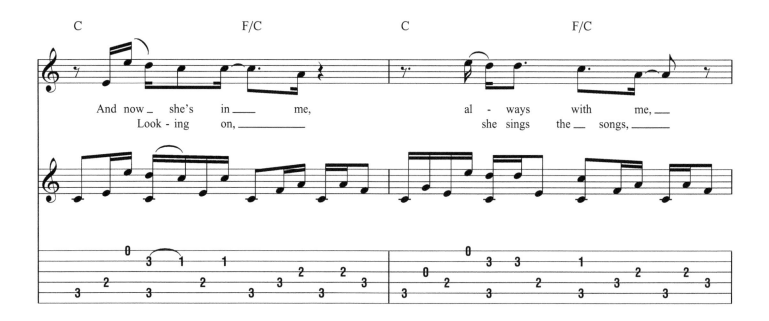

C   F/C   C   F/C

And now ___ she's in ___ me,   al - ways with me, ___
Look - ing on, ___   she sings the ___ songs, ___

C   G   Fsus2   C/E   D7sus4

ti - ny dan - cer in my hand. ___
the words ___ she knows, the tune she hums. ___

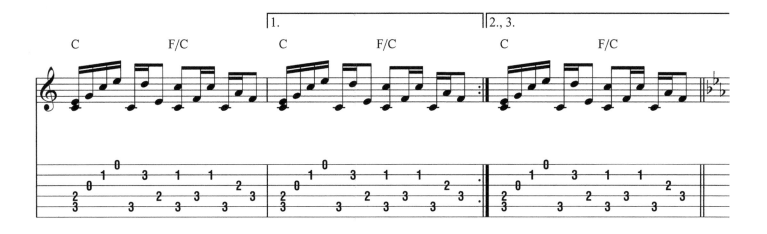

Bridge

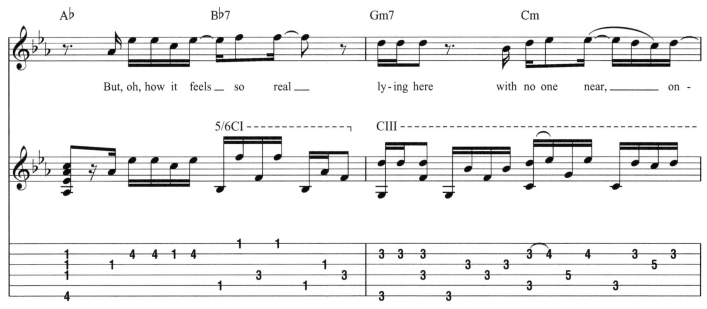

But, oh, how it feels __ so real __ ly-ing here with no one near, _____ on -

- ly you. And you __ can hear _____ me when I __ say

soft - ly, ___ slow - ly, ___

Chorus

"Hold me clos - er, ti - ny danc - er.

Count the head - lights on ___ the high - way. ___

Lay me down — in sheets — of lin - en.

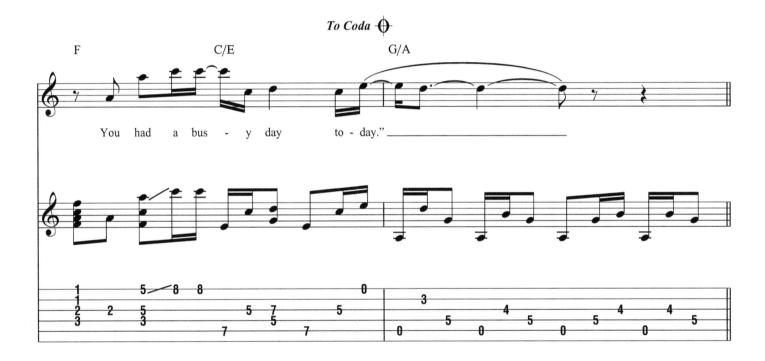

To Coda ⊕

You had a bus - y day to - day." ___

Interlude

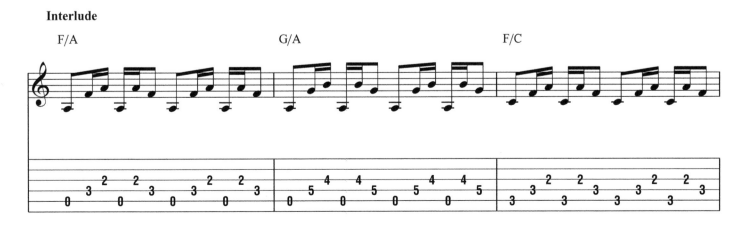

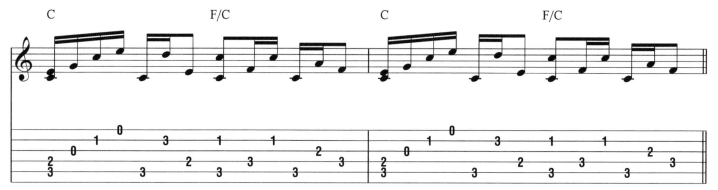

Coda

Outro

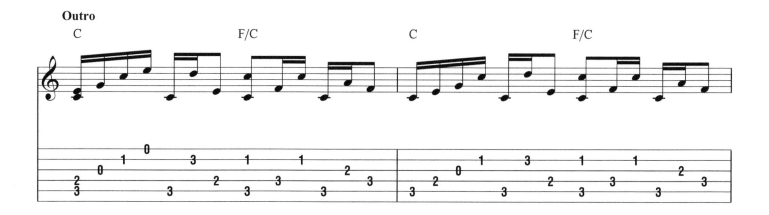

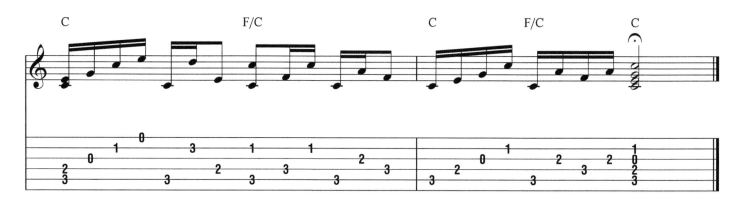

INTRODUCTION TO FINGERSTYLE GUITAR

Fingerstyle (a.k.a. fingerpicking) is a guitar technique that means you literally pick the strings with your right-hand fingers and thumb. This contrasts with the conventional technique of strumming and playing single notes with a pick (a.k.a. flatpicking). For fingerpicking, you can use any type of guitar: acoustic steel-string, nylon-string classical, or electric.

THE RIGHT HAND

The most common right-hand position is shown here.

Use a high wrist; arch your palm as if you were holding a ping-pong ball. Keep the thumb outside and away from the fingers, and let the fingers do the work rather than lifting your whole hand.

The thumb generally plucks the bottom strings with downstrokes on the left side of the thumb and thumbnail. The other fingers pluck the higher strings using upstrokes with the fleshy tip of the fingers and fingernails. The thumb and fingers should pluck one string per stroke and not brush over several strings.

Another picking option you may choose to use is called hybrid picking (a.k.a. plectrum-style fingerpicking). Here, the pick is usually held between the thumb and first finger, and the three remaining fingers are assigned to pluck the higher strings.

THE LEFT HAND

The left-hand fingers are numbered 1 through 4.

Be sure to keep your fingers arched, with each joint bent; if they flatten out across the strings, they will deaden the sound when you fingerpick. As a general rule, let the strings ring as long as possible when playing fingerstyle.

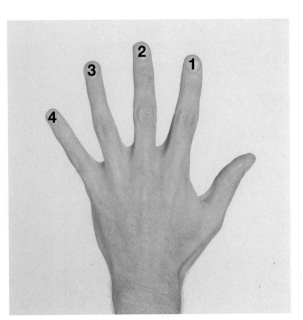

FINGERPICKING GUITAR BOOKS

Hone your fingerpicking skills with these great songbooks featuring solo guitar arrangements in standard notation and tablature. The arrangements in these books are carefully written for intermediate-level guitarists. Each song combines melody and harmony in one superb guitar fingerpicking arrangement. Each book also includes an introduction to basic fingerstyle guitar.

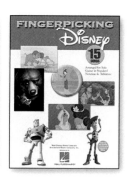

Fingerpicking Acoustic
00699614 15 songs......................$14.99

Fingerpicking Acoustic Classics
00160211 15 songs......................$16.99

Fingerpicking Acoustic Hits
00160202 15 songs......................$12.99

Fingerpicking Acoustic Rock
00699764 14 songs......................$14.99

Fingerpicking Ballads
00699717 15 songs......................$14.99

Fingerpicking Beatles
00699049 30 songs......................$24.99

Fingerpicking Beethoven
00702390 15 pieces......................$10.99

Fingerpicking Blues
00701277 15 songs......................$10.99

Fingerpicking Broadway Favorites
00699843 15 songs......................$9.99

Fingerpicking Broadway Hits
00699838 15 songs......................$7.99

Fingerpicking Campfire
00275964 15 songs......................$12.99

Fingerpicking Celtic Folk
00701148 15 songs......................$10.99

Fingerpicking Children's Songs
00699712 15 songs......................$9.99

Fingerpicking Christian
00701076 15 songs......................$12.99

Fingerpicking Christmas
00699599 20 carols......................$10.99

Fingerpicking Christmas Classics
00701695 15 songs......................$7.99

Fingerpicking Christmas Songs
00171333 15 songs......................$10.99

Fingerpicking Classical
00699620 15 pieces......................$10.99

Fingerpicking Country
00699687 17 songs......................$12.99

Fingerpicking Disney
00699711 15 songs......................$16.99

Fingerpicking Early Jazz Standards
00276565 15 songs......................$12.99

Fingerpicking Duke Ellington
00699845 15 songs......................$9.99

Fingerpicking Enya
00701161 15 songs......................$16.99

Fingerpicking Film Score Music
00160143 15 songs......................$12.99

Fingerpicking Gospel
00701059 15 songs......................$9.99

Fingerpicking Hit Songs
00160195 15 songs......................$12.99

Fingerpicking Hymns
00699688 15 hymns......................$12.99

Fingerpicking Irish Songs
00701965 15 songs......................$10.99

Fingerpicking Italian Songs
00159778 15 songs......................$12.99

Fingerpicking Jazz Favorites
00699844 15 songs......................$12.99

Fingerpicking Jazz Standards
00699840 15 songs......................$10.99

Fingerpicking Elton John
00237495 15 songs......................$14.99

Fingerpicking Latin Favorites
00699842 15 songs......................$12.99

Fingerpicking Latin Standards
00699837 15 songs......................$15.99

Fingerpicking Andrew Lloyd Webber
00699839 14 songs......................$16.99

Fingerpicking Love Songs
00699841 15 songs......................$14.99

Fingerpicking Love Standards
00699836 15 songs......................$9.99

Fingerpicking Lullabyes
00701276 16 songs......................$9.99

Fingerpicking Movie Music
00699919 15 songs......................$14.99

Fingerpicking Mozart
00699794 15 pieces......................$9.99

Fingerpicking Pop
00699615 15 songs......................$14.99

Fingerpicking Popular Hits
00139079 14 songs......................$12.99

Fingerpicking Praise
00699714 15 songs......................$14.99

Fingerpicking Rock
00699716 15 songs......................$14.99

Fingerpicking Standards
00699613 17 songs......................$14.99

Fingerpicking Wedding
00699637 15 songs......................$10.99

Fingerpicking Worship
00700554 15 songs......................$14.99

Fingerpicking Neil Young – Greatest Hits
00700134 16 songs......................$16.99

Fingerpicking Yuletide
00699654 16 songs......................$12.99

HAL•LEONARD®

Order these and more great publications from your favorite music retailer at
halleonard.com

Prices, contents and availability subject to change without notice.

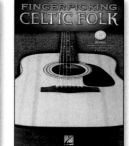

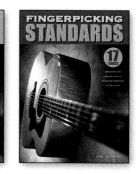

JAZZ GUITAR CHORD MELODY SOLOS

This series features chord melody arrangements in standard notation and tablature of songs for intermediate guitarists.

ALL-TIME STANDARDS

27 songs, including: All of Me • Bewitched • Come Fly with Me • A Fine Romance • Georgia on My Mind • How High the Moon • I'll Never Smile Again • I've Got You Under My Skin • It's De-Lovely • It's Only a Paper Moon • My Romance • Satin Doll • The Surrey with the Fringe on Top • Yesterdays • and more.
00699757 Solo Guitar $16.99

IRVING BERLIN

27 songs, including: Alexander's Ragtime Band • Always • Blue Skies • Cheek to Cheek • Easter Parade • Happy Holiday • Heat Wave • How Deep Is the Ocean • Puttin' On the Ritz • Remember • They Say It's Wonderful • What'll I Do? • White Christmas • and more.
00700637 Solo Guitar...........................$14.99

CHRISTMAS CAROLS

26 songs, including: Auld Lang Syne • Away in a Manger • Deck the Hall • God Rest Ye Merry, Gentlemen • Good King Wenceslas • Here We Come A-Wassailing • It Came upon the Midnight Clear • Joy to the World • O Holy Night • O Little Town of Bethlehem • Silent Night • Toyland • We Three Kings of Orient Are • and more.
00701697 Solo Guitar $14.99

CHRISTMAS JAZZ

21 songs, including Auld Lang Syne • Baby, It's Cold Outside • Cool Yule • Have Yourself a Merry Little Christmas • I've Got My Love to Keep Me Warm • Mary, Did You Know? • Santa Baby • Sleigh Ride • White Christmas • Winter Wonderland • and more.
00171334 Solo Guitar $15.99

DISNEY SONGS

27 songs, including: Beauty and the Beast • Can You Feel the Love Tonight • Candle on the Water • Colors of the Wind • A Dream Is a Wish Your Heart Makes • Heigh-Ho • Some Day My Prince Will Come • Under the Sea • When You Wish upon a Star • A Whole New World (Aladdin's Theme) • Zip-A-Dee-Doo-Dah • and more.
00701902 Solo Guitar $14.99

DUKE ELLINGTON

25 songs, including: C-Jam Blues • Caravan • Do Nothin' Till You Hear from Me • Don't Get Around Much Anymore • I Got It Bad and That Ain't Good • I'm Just a Lucky So and So • In a Sentimental Mood • It Don't Mean a Thing (If It Ain't Got That Swing) • Mood Indigo • Perdido • Prelude to a Kiss • Satin Doll • and more.
00700636 Solo Guitar $14.99

FAVORITE STANDARDS

27 songs, including: All the Way • Autumn in New York • Blue Skies • Cheek to Cheek • Don't Get Around Much Anymore • How Deep Is the Ocean • I'll Be Seeing You • Isn't It Romantic? • It Could Happen to You • The Lady Is a Tramp • Moon River • Speak Low • Take the "A" Train • Willow Weep for Me • Witchcraft • and more.
00699756 Solo Guitar...........................$16.99

JAZZ BALLADS

27 songs, including: Body and Soul • Darn That Dream • Easy to Love (You'd Be So Easy to Love) • Here's That Rainy Day • In a Sentimental Mood • Misty • My Foolish Heart • My Funny Valentine • The Nearness of You • Stella by Starlight • Time After Time • The Way You Look Tonight • When Sunny Gets Blue • and more.
00699755 Solo Guitar...........................$16.99

LATIN STANDARDS

27 Latin favorites, including: Água De Beber (Water to Drink) • Desafinado • The Girl from Ipanema • How Insensitive (Insensatez) • Little Boat • Meditation • One Note Samba (Samba De Uma Nota So) • Poinciana • Quiet Nights of Quiet Stars • Samba De Orfeu • So Nice (Summer Samba) • Wave • and more.
00699754 Solo Guitar...........................$14.99

Prices, content, and availability subject to change without notice.
Disney characters and artwork ™ & © 2021 Disney LLC

Order online at **halleonard.com**